GROUP DYNAMICS

HOW TO EFFECTIVELY HOLD A POSITIVE MEETING

by Frederick A. Marini

DORRANCE
PUBLISHING CO
EST. 1920
PITTSBURGH, PENNSYLVANIA 15238

Dorrance Publishing Co
585 Alpha Drive
Pittsburgh, PA 15238
Visit our website at *www.dorrancebookstore.com*

ISBN: 979-8-89499-274-7
eISBN: 979-8-89499-773-5

GROUP DYNAMICS

HOW TO EFFECTIVELY HOLD A POSITIVE MEETING

TABLE OF CONTENTS

INTRODUCTION:

Have you ever been in a group that gels and works effectively? Or have you found yourself in another group of people who can't seem to get started or stay on task?

Groups either work, or they don't, depending on the personalities of the individual members. Also, the size of a group can influence how individual personalities work or don't work together.

I'm about to share with you some secrets that I've learned over the years. Besides teaching for over 37 years and working with groups of students from grade school to high school, I've been on various committees and Boards (County, Regional, and State) and have seen excellent leadership and management styles. I've also seen personality disputes and many examples of what not to do.

For starters, you likely remember being assigned to a group for a school project. Often, if given a choice, this was with your friends.

Well, how well did that work out?

With your friends you have a common bond and likely your group got organized quickly.

Or, your group was quickly disorganized; depending on how little work your friends wanted to do and how easily distracted they were!

In schools and universities often good students dislike being in groups because they end up getting frustrated by the lack of effort from the rest of the group. Frequently they end up doing the bulk of the work while the other less than enthusiastic team members share the credit.

Well, welcome to the real world! This happens in business, government, the private sector, schools, church groups, and elsewhere in society. In this case "groups'" are often called committees, focus groups, board meetings, councils, Town Boards, etc.

With a better understanding of group roles and group dynamics, a better picture emerges that will help define the remaking and forming successful groups.

Think of it as putting a jigsaw puzzle together since not all the pieces fit when you try them at first, but in the end, the picture is clear.

So, unless you drop a few pieces on the floor you already know what the outcome should be based on your original goals and plans.

How you decide to put the jigsaw together involves various strategies:

- Do you start with the border?
- Do you group like colors together?
- Do you try to group parts of the puzzle together – buildings, flowers, etc.?
- Or, do you try to group the individual pieces by their design?

The following information and hints will give you a new perspective on "groups" and why some function well, while others fail.

CHAPTER 1: INDIVIDUAL CHARACTERISTICS

First, let's identify two types of people: Introverts and Extroverts

- Extroverts are often perceived as leaders since they
    - Are open
    - Are easy to get along with
    - Talkative
    - They are comfortable in front of people
        - They easily make small talk and thus seem socially adept
    - They like an audience
        - Extroverts enjoy social situations and enjoy being around people
        - This is because other people invigorate extroverts
    - They tend to think best when talking
        - Reflecting on concepts doesn't seem as real unless they can talk about them
    - Extroverts get easily bored without people around and tend to "diminish" when alone
- Introverts are
    - Often appear shyer
    - Quiet
    - Like to work alone
    - They get energized by being alone
    - They tend to think before they speak
    - Are often not as comfortable in front of others
        - This depends on the size of the group
        - It also depends on if they know some of the group
    - They fade into the background without meaning too
    - But, by no means are they any less capable of being an effective leader!

Where do you fit into the above?

It is also possible that you may change over time with practice and experience depending on the group. As an Introvert you may find that in a comfortable surrounding with friends, you are more outgoing and talkative. Gee, starting to sound like you are a bit of an "Extrovert".

So, what has changed?

- Your personal environment

Being with your friends has made you more comfortable and led to this shift.

- There are other factors that may draw you out as well.

Perhaps a topic of high interest helps you to be more verbal (and you may not even notice the change).

Maybe a favorite TV show, music performer, sport, book, or movie being mentioned piques your interest.

Often hot topics like abortion, the death penalty, deer hunting, cruelty to animals, as well as many others can set off a frenzy of heated discussions.

CHAPTER 2: GROUP BEHAVIOR

Why do some groups work and others don't? For starters remember that we are all individuals and as such we often carry a lot of baggage around with us to work, school, business, meetings, and so forth. (And I'm not talking about briefcases, purses, or backpacks!)

When you get to work, school, or your meetings do you:

- Feel tired

- Didn't get enough sleep last night
- Feel hungry
- Forgot something at home
- Had car trouble

- Are you running late
- Got in an argument at home (and it is still festering)

- Have sick people at home or other worries
- Maybe you aren't feeling the best

CHAPTER 3: NOW MEET THE PEOPLE YOU WILL BE WORKING WITH

Types of People in a Group – Which describes you best?

Hint: You may need to check several.

- ☐ Take charge kind of person
- ☐ Quiet / reserved
- ☐ Good listener
- ☐ "Yes" person
- ☐ Follower, not necessarily a "yes person"
- ☐ Organized
- ☐ Takes great notes
- ☐ Likes to talk
- ☐ Likes to debate
- ☐ Argues
- ☐ Antagonizes Others
- ☐ Likes to hear themselves talk
- ☐ Makes quality statements
- ☐ Positive
- ☐ Negative
- ☐ Works well with others
- ☐ Works best alone
- ☐ Leadership – backed with experience
- ☐ Leadership – new at this
- ☐ First time at this meeting – unsure of role and duties
- ☐ Well informed
- ☐ Biased
- ☐ Unbiased
- ☐ Has hidden agendas
- ☐ Carries a grudge
- ☐ Carries lots of personal/emotional baggage & can't stay focused on the meeting
- ☐ Has a sense of humor
- ☐ Takes criticisms well
- ☐ Can't take criticism
- ☐ Accomplished speaker
- ☐ Nervous in front of others
- ☐ Likes to stay in the background, but has great ideas
- ☐ Works best in small groups
- ☐ Sociable
- ☐ Anti-social
- ☐ Intelligent
- ☐ I don't know why I was selected
- ☐ I have trouble hearing
- ☐ I have trouble seeing
- ☐ I have trouble following what's going on
- ☐ Who are these people? Am I at the right meeting?
- ☐ Historian / Been on this Board or committee before and knows the history of past issues and debates
- ☐ Wordsmith – good at phrasing motions
- ☐ Great negotiator – can get different sides together to form a consensus
- ☐ Great moderator – keeps the meeting focused and on task. Also, lets everyone have the chance to speak!
- ☐ Pain in the #*%. We've all met these people, but are you one of them?
- ☐ Proficient in "Robert's Rules of Order" and Parliamentary Law
- ☐ Great at summarizing statements and details
- ☐ Good mathematician – helpful with budgets and data analysis

- ☐ Likes to volunteer – glad to be on other committees
- ☐ Allergies to people's perfume, cologne, cigarette smell, etc. that distract from the meeting
- ☐ Thirsty
- ☐ Likes to snack
- ☐ Drinks too much coffee
- ☐ Needs to drink coffee to wake up
- ☐ Forgets to turn off their cell phone
- ☐ Finds the room too hot or too cold - not much air ventilation
- ☐ Overdazzled by the boss, big names/major players on the board
- ☐ Not paying attention - more interested in an attractive person at the meeting.
- ☐ Sloppy appearance
- ☐ Well dressed
- ☐ Overdressed for the occasion (may depend on the type of meeting and audience present).
- ☐ Needs a haircut
- ☐ Needs breath mints
- ☐ Has an annoying laugh, clears throat, annoying cough …
- ☐ Talks too soft
- ☐ Talks too loud - overpowering
- ☐ Are you speaking English? Can't understand what you are saying.
- ☐ Uses too much jargon - not everyone may understand.
- ☐ Likes to impress people - may leave phone on to get calls to let groups think they are busy and important.
- ☐ Has an annoying voice to listen to.

1. **How many of the above did you check for yourself?**
2. **How many of the above did you recognize for other people in your group, or for past groups?**

Lesson One

When I was teaching, I challenged students to work effectively in groups.

- First: I split the students up into groups of five people.
- Then I created badges that two students from each group hung around their necks.
- All groups were assigned the same task and each group had ten minutes to try to come up with an answer.
    - The first badge was randomly assigned to someone to be the LEADER.
    - The second badge was the RECORDER. This person would read the task and ask if everyone understood it.
    - Each group had ten minutes to solve the task.
    - That was it. The recorder could no longer speak or take part in the group (no matter how much they wanted).
- The RECORDER'S job was to LISTEN and take notes on the following:
    - How quickly did the group get organized?
    - Who took charge of the group?
        - How long did that last?
        - Did someone else try to dominate the group?
    - Did the group stay on task?
    - Who controlled the group?
        - Was it the appointed LEADER?
    - Did the group work together or did it split apart?
        - Reasons: Why? Who offended someone…
    - Who felt <u>uncomfortable</u> in the group or stood to the side and let others talk?
    - Did everyone listen to people's ideas?
    - Who was the best at working out strategies?
    - Who gave the best directions?
    - Who drifted into daydreaming doing this group exercise?
    - Did the group use any resources?
    - Who took part in the discussion?
        - All

- Some
- A small few

- Who had great ideas and was helpful?
  - Did people listen or push them aside?
- Who got off track?
  - Wasted time?
  - Wanted to hear themselves talk?
- Who would not listen?
  - Why?
- Who didn't take part?
  - Why?
- Who dominated the discussion?
  - Was it helpful or not?
- Was the group successful in solving the task?
- If not, why?

The results were eye-openers!

1. The recorders were frustrated that they couldn't take part, especially when the group was led in a distracting tangent.
2. They easily spotted the leader (this was an iffy term in some groups).

- Many times, this was not the person assigned this task.
- The assigned leader didn't know what to do.
- They relinquished their role to a more dominant person. Sometimes this was a big mistake.

3. One frustrated recorder pointed out that the leader in their group ignored the one person who had the right answer.
   - This person was shut down and dropped out.
   - They were upset that their idea did not count.
   - They were embarrassed and mad.
   - This person of course was proved right when their group failed to complete the task. They could have won within the first minute if they had respected and listened to all their group members.

Types of people you may be dealing with:

The Know-it-alls: They can be arrogant and usually have an opinion on every issue. When they are wrong, they get defensive.

The Unresponsive: These people never offer ideas or let you know where they stand.

The Bully: They harass and intimidate. They are constantly demanding and are brutally critical of opinions that differ from their way of thinking. They take offense at any challenge to their ideas.

The "Yes" people: They agree to any commitment but don't always deliver. You can't always trust them to follow through.

The "No" people: They are quick to point out why something will not work. They are often uncompromising.

The Complainers and Grumblers: To these people, nothing is ever right. They prefer to complain rather than find solutions.

CHAPTER 4: HOW INDIVIDUALS THINK AND RESPOND

So far what I am alluding to is that we have all taken part in groups, committees, and meetings but how often has anyone been trained in how to better utilize the variations found in group dynamics?

For example: when doing jigsaw puzzles do you think in terms of colors or images, etc.? Or, if I tear apart a computer can you make sense out of what you see inside? Verbally hearing the words may shoot right past you without much sense without a visual connection. Seeing something demonstrated along with written or verbal cues may work better for you. But what about those individuals that you are working with in your group?

The above descriptions fit the study of Howard Garner relating to his theory of "Multiple Intelligences and Learning". He has isolated 9 theories thus far. Note that many universities offer courses in his Theory of Multiple Intelligences work. But not all agree with him. He has been critiqued for never having his theories tested or being subjected to peer evaluation. I would disagree since his work has been tested and accepted for several generations.

Perhaps a better explanation is that it is "common sense" and can't always be pigeonholed into set categories. Specific tests for intelligence and IQ tests, Gardner argues only take into account linguistic, logical, and mathematical intelligence.

You might note that these intelligences are often the way we have been taught and are continually being educated. Some people excel at this while others have problems or don't fully understand.

As a retired teacher I could often spot these people so I changed things up in group tasks and individual tasks. I put the emphasis on more of the other 6 intelligences (Musical, Interpersonal, Intrapersonal, Natural, Bodily-Kinetics, and Existential) rather than based solely on Language, Math, or Logic.

Suddenly the world flipped! My straight "A" students were confused and had problems with the tasks. My not caring, never turning in homework, always visiting (and not on topic), and hating school (except for sports and lunch) had finished the tasks in nothing flat. WOW! They even got them right, understood them, and asked if there were more.....

Not totally expecting this I thought fast as I looked at these "C" and "F" scoring students. I realized I had evened the playing field and they soared to the front while the "A" students were frustrated and embarrassed. So, I flipped their world again and asked these newly rejuvenated students if they would like to team up with students ("A" kids) and work with them. Surprising smiles resulted in "Yes". They were no longer an underdog but were equal to their peers. The results worked again. This opened up the class to asking questions and true learning went up a notch.

So, what are these intelligences or "common sense" learning styles?

Verbal/Linguistic Intelligence

- This is the person who likes language, reading, and/or writing.
- This intelligence includes the ability to successfully use language to articulate oneself orally or in writing.
- They have the ability to understand the spoken and written language.
    - This can sometimes be irritating to others or it can impress people with this ability.
- They often have the desire and skill to learn foreign languages.
    - They can speak and read this language.
- They understand the meaning and grammar of these languages.
- People with Verbal/Linguistic Intelligence may use mnemonics (memory word tricks) or acronyms to memorize written information.
- People with this type of intelligence can be overly sensitive to

criticism or sarcastic remarks.

- They can use justifications, pretexts, and other reasons to make their skillful point that water is not wet or their dog ate their homework
- Types of people this intelligence might apply:
    - Speakers
    - Writers
    - Poets
    - Lawyers
    - Novelists
    - Journalists
    - Storytelling
    - People that like doing crossword puzzles
    - People that like doing reports

Logical-Mathematical Intelligence

- These people prefer a high degree of organization in a group situation or in a structured classroom.
- Usually not comfortable in chaotic settings.
- Likely to be computer literate.
- They are analytical and are thought of as being rational.
- Logical-Mathematical people are at ease in doing math, seeing patterns, working out strategies, seeing patterns, working on strategy games, thinking deductively, and working logically.
- Their work has a progression that they can understand and make sense out of.
- This is the main way in which education focuses on learning when we are taught.
- If you don't have this type of focused "Intelligence" you are distracted, your mind wanders, and you have trouble understanding the directives of the tasks.
- The following are typical descriptions of this intelligence:
    - Like to solve math problems.
    - Distinguish relationships and connections.
    - Understand propositions and hypotheses.
    - They use abstract representational thought and sequential

reasoning.
    - They use inductive and deductive thinking.
    - They are interested in patterns.
- Types of people this intelligence might apply:
    - Mathematicians
    - Scientists
    - Program Designers
    - Computer Technicians
    - Detectives

Bodily-Kinesthetic Intelligence

- People with this intelligence love movement. They have good motor skills.
- The athlete! Okay, not everyone fits into this athletic intelligence. These people have the capability of using their body (or hands, feet, legs…) skillfully. We see this in athletes, dancers, actors, and other sports stars. But it includes more … This can involve hand-eye coordination in doing crafts, woodworking, and other similar skills.
- Bodily-kinesthetic intelligence requires the ability to use one's whole body or parts of the body to solve problems. It is the ability to use mental abilities to coordinate bodily movements.
- The following are typical descriptions of this intelligence:
    - Well-coordinated with quality motor skills.
    - They are good at building things.
    - They are aware of their bodies and coordinated.
    - They learn through movement and experimentation.
    - They like to be active.
    - They have a lot of physical energy.
    - They can't sit still for long periods of time.
    - They enjoy sports and stimulating experiences
    - They learn by doing and figuring out how things work.
- Types of people this intelligence might apply:
    - Athlete
    - Dancer
    - Actor/Actress

- Performer
- Carpenter
- Farmer
- Physical Therapist
- Firefighter
- Paramedic
- Surgeons
- Craftspeople

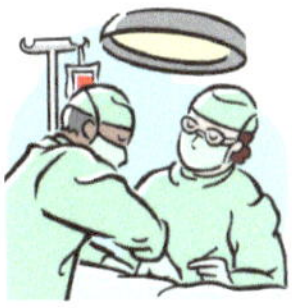

Please note:

- These people may also have difficulty sitting still for long periods of time.
- They likely will remember what is done rather than what is said.
- They may easily be distracted by others moving about.

Visual / Spatial Intelligence

- These people are good at visualizing things.
- They are good with maps, charts, pictures, and video images.
- Are you better at visualizing something rather than reading directions or being given verbal audible directions? Simply put if you can see something visually demonstrated do you understand it better? Examples would be drawing,
- The following are typical descriptions of this intelligence:
    - Enjoys reading and writing.
    - Good at putting puzzles together.
    - Good at interpreting pictures, graphs, and charts.
    - Enjoys drawing, painting, and the visual arts.
    - Recognizes patterns easily.
    - Think in three dimensions
    - Mental imagery
    - Image manipulation
    - Active imagination
    - Daydreaming
- Types of people this intelligence might apply:
    - Sailors
    - Pilots

- Painters
- Sculptors
- Architect
- Artist
- Engineer

Musical Intelligence

- Pretty much tells it all! Some people just naturally like to sing, hum, or tap their fingers to an unheard song in their head. Music is a major part of their awareness. They are likely to pick out sounds and rhythms before others are aware of them, even if they are only in the background.
- Musical intelligence involves an appreciation for musical patterns plus the skill in performance and composition. This intelligence encompasses the competence to recognize tones, pitches, and rhythms.
- They also have a Logical-Mathematical link.
- People with Musical intelligence have the ability to understand the intentions, motivations, and even desires of other people. It helps them to work effectively with others.
- They have a strong appreciation for music and are good at musical composition, directing, and performance.
- The following are typical descriptions of this intelligence:
    - Enjoy singing and playing musical instruments.
    - Recognizes musical patterns and tones easily.
    - Good at remembering songs and melodies.
    - Rich understanding of musical structure, rhythm, and notes.
- Types of people this intelligence might apply:
    - Musician
    - Composer
    - Singer
    - Music Teacher
    - Conductor

Interpersonal Intelligence

- It involves how skillful an individual is in understanding and dealing with others. Individuals who excel in this intelligence typically are able to discern the moods, feelings, and motivations of others. Politicians, teachers, and counselors are among those that Howard Gardner sees as having high interpersonal intelligence.
- Although Gardner classifies interpersonal and intrapersonal intelligences separately, there is a lot of interplay between the two and they are often grouped together.
- The following are typical descriptions of this intelligence:
    - Interpersonal Intelligence is concerned with the ability to understand the intentions, motivations, and desires of other people. It allows people to work effectively with others.
- Types of people this intelligence might apply:
    - Counselors
    - Social workers
    - Salespeople
    - Educators
    - Religious leaders
    - Political leaders

Examples include Gandhi, Ronald Reagan, and Bill Clinton

Note:

Learns best when allowed to interact with others.

This includes group work and cooperative activities.

Enjoys cooperative learning, peer editing, and team-building activities.

Intrapersonal Intelligence

- This is a person with an Intuitive intelligence that has the ability to access, understand, and communicate one's own inner feelings.
- Can be a very private person.
- Contains self-knowledge.
- Is deeply aware of one's own feelings.
- Has a strong awareness of one's purpose in life.
- Is self-motivated.
- Has a well-developed sense of self.
- Is willing to go against the grain.

- Is also willing to mediate arguments.
- Has sensitivity to others.
- Recognizing others' moods and temperaments.
- Has an understanding of other people.
- Has a keen awareness of others' feelings and motives.
- Is Introspective.
- The following are typical descriptions of this intelligence:
    - Likes to make time for contemplation and reflection.
    - Likes to do independent study.
    - Follows their intuition.
    - Likes to schedule debriefing sessions to clarify their own thinking.
- Types of people this intelligence might apply:
    - Psychologists
    - Spiritual leaders/religious
    - Educators/teachers
    - Counselors
    - Social Workers
    - Salespeople
    - Philosophers
    - Political Leaders/politicians
    - Actors
    - Novelists
    - Song Writers

Note: Intrapersonal People

- Needs wait time to respond to questions and reflect on learning.
- Responds well to empowerment activities with choices in assignments.
- Likes journals or writing notebooks for personal thoughts.
- Discusses and/or writes about their experiences.
- Likes to take control of their own learning.
- Uses questions to gain clarity of self.
- Likes to read.
- May be a doodler. They can often multi-task and are likely listening while they doodle.
- Can often be handicapped if challenged by only using print-only items

or doing long assignments.

- Likes to visualize learning concepts.

Author's Note:

- I would associate what I called earlier "Introverts" into this intelligence. While everything may not quite fit exactly, many do fit.
- Remember that a person may have one or more of "Gardner's Multiple Intelligences". However, some may not be as dominant.

Naturalist Intelligence

- Naturalist intelligence are individuals who are more in tune with nature. They are interested in exploring the environment, nurturing, and learning about other species.
- These people are highly aware of their environment and any subtle changes in it.
- According to Gardner, this theory has also been met with more resistance than the other intelligences.
- The following are typical descriptions of this intelligence:
    - May enjoy camping, gardening, hiking, and exploring the outdoors.
    - Good at categorizing and cataloging information easily.
    - Interested in subjects such as botany, biology, and zoology.
    - Doesn't enjoy learning unfamiliar topics that have no connection to nature.
- Types of people this intelligence might apply:
    - Gardener
    - Biologist
    - Conservationist
    - Farmer

Note:

- These people learn best when knowledge is linked/connected to past experiences/topics.
- They pay attention to minute details, relationships, and sensory information.

Existential Intelligence

- Gardner also considered calling this 'moral' intelligence, and has not developed this type very extensively; it receives little mention, or attention, in other articles on Gardner's theory of multiple intelligences.
- Intelligence is used to understand the larger fundamental questions of existence.
- They have a firm understanding of their own personal beliefs, preferences, and convictions.
- They are frequently motivated and good at evaluating their own work.
- These people enjoy school activities that allow them a choice of activities.
- The following are typical descriptions of this intelligence:
  - People with this intelligence prefer to express themselves and their opinions as opposed to memorizing facts and information.
  - They prefer to act on their opinions.
  - They enjoy managing their own learning and are good at evaluating their own performance.
  - They work well independently and are motivated to do well.
- Types of people this intelligence might apply:
  - Counselors
  - Psychologists / Psychiatrist
  - Motivational speakers
  - Social workers
  - Independent business workers
  - Philosopher
  - Ministry
  - Theoretical scientist

Note:

- People with this intelligence may have difficulty conforming to others' expectations.
- They may also have problems accepting their own mistakes.

So, by now you are starting to feel like the picture below.

Don't worry, try these simple steps first:

1. Reread the above intelligences and see where you fit.
2. As you do this mentally put some of your co-workers and friends into the above,
3. Remember back to past meetings you were part of
   a. Which ones worked?
   b. Which ones failed?
   c. Which involved arguments?
   d. Can you imagine the attributes of the people involved and can you see which intelligences meshed and which pushed "Hot Buttons" in others?

Now, don't get too comfortable….

I would also add one of my own…

Cultural/Heritage Intelligence:

Your personal background has a major influence on your behavior. In some cultures, it is impolite to look into someone's eyes when addressing them. It is viewed as being rude and challenging. In others, this is common and expected. Looking away with downcast eyes often signals distrust, lying, or other implications.

Acceptable and common hand gestures in one culture may be an insult in another culture. Some cultures shake hands, some kiss on the cheeks, some bow.

Where this is leading is KNOW YOUR AUDIENCE! This is a basic communication rule.

- Whom are you talking to - do you have a common culture with acceptable norms.

- Are you meeting in a distant location, perhaps in a foreign country on business?
  - With the Internet, Skype, Go-to-Meetings, etc. you might be meeting online rather than face-to-face in person.
  - If so, research and know the cultural differences and beliefs before sticking your foot in your mouth and destroying any chance you have of a business deal or association.
- Accept the fact that people's heritage and comfort levels are different. What may seem like a casual meeting for you may seem unorganized or painfully rude to another.
- Also, accept the fact that not everyone is going to agree and see things in the same manner that you see them.
- This is okay as long as you are not placing blame.
- Work with it and accept it as a challenge.
- How can you adapt to the situation and get people working together with a common purpose?

There are actually professionally trained people who will put on organizational meetings. But with a little background and training on your own, you will be better qualified to do this yourself, without having to hire consultants or having to outsource your training.

Just to add fuel to the mix I should mention that each of us also learns differently. This has a major impact as to how well groups get along and listen to each other.

Just to make life more complex you might as well figure that a person can fall into several of these categories. Even then you may see yourself differently than your close friends see you!

By now you are probably saying "Ok, so what?"

The "what" is that once people see how this starts to come together, they make startling discoveries! I've had students tell me "Oh, so that's why our group didn't work together so well". Yes, internal group conflict can easily result in a lack of focus, anger, frustration, and arguments.

Throughout all this, you witness that nothing is clear cut. Especially since we may have two or more favorite intelligences.

However, knowing the above helps you plan better and allows you to tap into your individual group member strengths.

Remember that in your educational training, the bulk of your learning was taught mostly in terms of Linguistic Intelligence and Logical-Mathematical Intelligence. But, please remember that these intelligences are not learning styles. They are how individuals perceive, think, and react. Knowing this opens up possibilities for having success with groups.

This may not have been the best way to teach you and you may have struggled or felt frustrated. The same often happens in groups.

If you're a Linguistic and/or Logical-Mathematical person, a Visual/Spatial person, who loves to daydream, will drive the group nuts, and will be hard to keep on task. Is this bad - not always, as it invites creative dialogue and out-of-the-box ideas.

If you are with like-minded learners, things can often go smoother and you can accomplish your tasks quicker. Might you have done better in school if you had a choice in how you were being taught? Definitely yes!

How do you fit in?

What combinations work best for you?

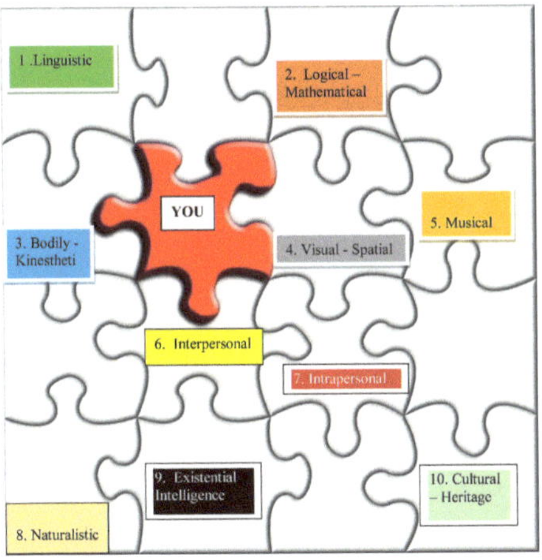

1. When you are in a group do you shy away?	7
2. When you are with friends do you lead the conversation?	6
3. Do others see you as a leader?	6
4. Do you sing to yourself?	5
5. Are you more comfortable outdoors than indoors?	8
6. Do you like to do jigsaw puzzles?	4
7. Do you daydream a lot?	4
8. Are you athletic?	3
9. Do you like to tell stories?	1
10. Do you have fun doing crossword puzzles?	1
11. Do you like math?	2
12. Do you like to do woodworking?	3
13. Are you aware of others' feelings?	6
14. Is it easier to think in terms of colors and images?	4
15. Do you like to work by yourself?	7
16. Do you like to read?	1
17. Do you often hear sounds others may miss?	5
18. Do you like to dance?	3
19. Are you good at motivating others?	6
20. Do you like to keep a diary or journal?	1
21. Are you big on excuses?	1
22. Are you overly sensitive to criticism and sarcastic remarks?	1
23. Do you use mnemonics to memorize information?	1
24. Do you prefer a high degree of organization and a structured classroom	2
25. Does a chaotic setting drive you nuts and makes you uncomfortable	2
26. Are you meeting with a group of business leaders via Skye in Japan?	10
27. Do you tend to be more computer literate?	2
28. Do you need to visualize your learning?	4

29. Do you doodle a lot at meetings? 4

30. Do you have high sensitivity to sounds, voices, rhythmic patterns? 5

31. Do you tap your fingers, hum, or whisper when the room is quiet? 5

32. Do you have trouble sitting for long periods of time? 3

33. Are you easily distracted by movement of other people 3

34. Do you remember the outcomes of a meeting more than what was said? 3

35. Do you pay attention to minute details? 8

36. Do you learn best when you use prior knowledge? 8

36. Do you learn best when you are allowed to interact with others? 6

38. Do you enjoy cooperative learning, team building activities? 6

39. Do you like to write in notebooks or journals for personal reflections? 7

40. Do you prefer your opinion over other people's facts? 9

41. Do you like to have time to think before responding to questions? 7

42. Do you like to be able to choose your own assignments? 7

43. If meeting with foreign dignitaries and someone makes a hand gesture - do you know if this is a good sign or a sign of disrespect? 10

1. Where do you fit into the above puzzle?
2. Does this affect how you learn?
3. Does this relate to how well you function in a group?
4. Do others view you in the same way you view yourself?
5. Have you worked with others that match any of the above descriptions?
6. Do you see several combinations that represent you?
   If so, some may be more dominant in one setting than in others depending on the group you are in, your situation, and how comfortable you are. Example: At work vs with friends.
7. Are there some types that you just don't understand?
   If so, this may present a working barrier as you would not be able to mentally put yourself into their shoes.

Note: You may actually fit into several of the above categories.

CHAPTER 5: GROUP LEADER / FACILITATOR

- Selection
  - Sometimes this person is appointed to this role.
  - Sometimes this person is elected to this position.
    - Associations, clubs, boards
  - If work related it may be your boss, a manager, or a department head.
  - If none of the above apply (example: school groups, committees) then:
    - Ask for a volunteer
    - If more than one volunteers (or if no one wants the job)
      - Vote
      - Draw names
- Roll of the Group Leader / Facilitator
  - Know what your complete task for the group is all about before you start.
    - If in doubt ask so that you can inform your group.
  - Be positive.
    - Set a rule that all ideas will be listened to.
    - Inform the group that while there can be disagreements, there will be no fighting, arguments, backstabbing, negative put-downs, etc.
    - A State Organizational Board that I was on once started our first session by giving everybody a coupon.
    - It was a "Free Pass / I Made a Mistake" coupon. If you goofed you presented this "one-time coupon" so no one would get mad or condemn you. It opened up people to more creative thinking and ideas.

  - Keep the meeting on track.
    - Start on time! End on time!
    - People get annoyed if they've busted their butts getting to the meeting on time only to have to wait for latecomers to

show up. This destroys your credibility and encourages this to happen again and again.

    - Latecomers will have to deal with being late and left out at the beginning of the session. They will learn that your "Start time" is the actual START TIME you begin.
    - I also try to set an "End time" and stick to it. People may have to drive a long distance, pick up kids from school, make lunch for their family, or need to go to another meeting.
- Get everyone involved to participate.
- Help reach a group consensus and decision regarding the recommendations for the outcome of your task.
- A facilitator also has to take on a neutral role at times so that all viewpoints can be fairly examined.
    - You may have your own personal views but remember your task and that this is a group decision and not yours alone!
- You may have to set up future meeting dates.
    - If so, pick dates that work for your group or committee.
    - Realize that not everyone can meet and that you may have to compromise to get the greatest number of people present.
    - If you are meeting often, you may want to pick a standard date and time (example: Tuesdays at 10:00 A.M.; first Thursday of the month at 6:00 pm; etc.)
- You will also be responsible for setting your meeting agendas.
    - Make sure your group has this ahead of time to read and digest, to jot down questions, or call people if information is needed.
    - In today's digital world, this can be sent by e-mail, providing you have everyone's correct e-mail address, or by regular mail.
        - Remember some groups differ in age and not everyone has a computer or wants one.
- Addition hints for the Facilitator / Group Leader:
    - Keep the meeting focused on your topic/task.
        - Sometimes conversations get off-topic or take strange directions. You are responsible for getting people back on topic.

        - Sometimes you just have to interrupt and say, "I'm sorry but we're getting off-topic" or "We're getting sidetracked and need to get back on task".
        - Hint: In some larger groups a person may be assigned the task of timekeeper to keep discussions to a set time limit per topic.
    - Accept all ideas and individual contributions
    - To make sure you understand lengthy discussions or unclear statements, summarize or clarify what's been said:
        - Restate the problem in a different way is often a great help in understanding what has been said.
        - If you don't understand something
            - Ask the person to explain what they mean.
            - Again, rephrase what's been said… "If I understand what you've said correctly, you would ….."
                - If this isn't correct, they can clarify what they mean
        - It is helpful in larger groups to have members signal when they want to talk by raising their hand. The Facilitator / Group Leader then calls on specific individuals to speak.
            - This avoids people getting cut off or someone out shouting for someone else to be heard.
            - If someone hasn't finished their say, come back to that person and say, "I'm sorry you were cut off before you finished. Is there anything else that you might like to add?"
    - Know when the discussion needs to move to a new topic and then do it.
- Avoid pitfalls
    - Put a limit on lengthy comments, or interrupt the person and tell them you understand what they are saying and that the group/committee needs to move on.
    - Watch for emotions as some topics may hit "hot buttons" and set people off. Step in immediately and control the tone of the meeting!

        - Accept that some emotions are necessary.
        - Avoid arguments.
        - Don't criticize or put down someone's ideas or comments – you can still disagree but in a positive manner.
        - If needed, follow Robert's Rules of Order for procedural decisions. At least use a loose form of this procedure to keep everything running smoothly and consistently.
        - Sometimes you get someone (or more) who likes to dominate, you can lose control of your meeting/group quickly if you don't make it clear that you are in charge.
    - How to get peoples' attention to start a meeting.
        - Ever been to a meeting when the leader has trouble getting everyone's attention because they are still socializing? If you are lucky, someone in the crowd has that loud piercing whistle that gets everyone's attention (while the leader looks frustrated.)
            - Use a gavel
            - Ring a bell
            - Be creative, try a duck call
            - Play a bit of music
            - Use a whistle
            - Use a "leftover" New Year's noise maker
            - Dim the lights
            - Please don't use the microphone feedback to create that annoying high-pitch.
            - Think back to other meetings and see what others have done.

CHAPTER 6: HOW TO GET TEAM MEMBERS MORE INVOLVED

1. Work with the strengths of your distinctive leadership style.
   a. Observe other people that you know are great leaders.
   b. Read books on leadership.

2. Make members aware of "unwritten rules or policies" and/or "Code of conduct".
3. Maintain a personal and professional balance so you remain the leader while still being part of the team.
   a. This lets everyone know <u>you are in charge</u>.
   b. If you fail at this you become wishy-washy and will have problems, especially if others think you are playing favoritism.

4. Be positive – this will help improve everyone's self-esteem.
   a. SMILE – This is the easiest way to stay positive and look confident.
   b. Call people by names – it makes them feel important and a useful part of the team.

   c. Listen when others are talking.
      i. Don't browse through your e-mail.
      ii. Don't get in conversations with others when someone is talking.
   d. Thank people and praise them for their work and ideas. You will be surprised at how much more work they will do to support you.
   e. Give people the chance to succeed.
      i. No amount of work should be unappreciated.
      ii. Constantly offer up encouragement.
   f. If someone missed a meeting, welcome them back and let them know they were missed.
   g. By doing the above you offer people the chance to take part of the ownership of the group's task.
      i. They will take a more active role in the work needed to be done.

ii. Proactive followers will prove their value for the success of your team.

iii. This empowerment will make them part of the solution.

5. Learn to understand people often have <u>hidden agendas</u> that can sabotage a meeting.
    a. Let people know they all carry baggage but it should be left at the door. Examples:
        i. Internal politics.
        ii. Differing viewpoint.
        iii. One-upmanship.
        iv. Feuds and backbiting end now!
        v. Using the meeting as a placeholder to look good on a resume.

6. If you disagree with someone let them know it is <u>not personal.</u>
    a. Explain to them your reasons so that they may understand. They may not agree with you but they will respect you.
    b. Sometimes they don't see or understand the bigger picture. Let them expand their horizons and let them in on your thinking.
    c. It is also a good way for them to save face.

7. Be consistent at your meetings. <u>Watch for more specific details in the next chapter.</u>
8. Make team meetings more time-efficient, productive experiences.
    a. Avoid business jargon until you are sure everyone understands what you are talking about:

Synergy	Best Practices	Bottom Line
Benchmark	Value-Added	Knowledge Based
Leverage	Client Focused	Result Driven
24/7	Empower	Mindset

    Acronyms – Make sure all know what they are
    b. Don't ask people to raise their hands if they don't know specific jargon. It is embarrassing to be signaled out and will make people look stupid.
9. Turn your visions into action plans focused on achieving specific goals.

a. As a former teacher, we are constantly taught this and are always working to improve our skills.
b. Read up on this topic for more information and practice.

10. Develop communication skills that help you "connect" with team members.
    a. This includes sending out notices and agendas prior to the meeting.
    b. Following up with assigned committees.
    c. Following up on any promises (calling others, doing deeper research, etc.) made at the meeting.
    d. Letting members know what is happening and any progress that is made.
        i. Letters
        ii. E-mail
        iii. Twitter
        iv. Or any other useful electronic/digital use. Remember ALL members must be able to have access to whatever you use! If not, they will feel left out and you will have to split your group.
11. Learn how to delegate work.
    a. You can't do it all by yourself!
        i. If you do, you get too close and won't be able to see the trees for the forest.

        ii. It lessens stress in your life.
        iii. It empowers others to lead, along with your guidance and support.
        iv. Above all, set time limits for committees.
            1. This lets them know it is not for life.
            2. If the committee isn't working out (keep reading this book to figure out why) make subtle changes without disrupting the delegated work.
12. Keep notes on your team members.
    a. Get to know their birthday, their anniversary, if their kids play sports, etc.

b. At the start of the meeting give positive acknowledgement of their accomplishments and family successes.

c. This is a good way for people to make connections in order to work cooperatively with one another.

13. Know when to hold your ground or if you can compromise for the success of your mission.
14. All of this helps you project an image of professionalism and self-confidence.
    a. These skills will be noticed and most likely copied by others.
    b. You will learn strategies for working with people that will benefit you in the future.

CHAPTER 7: EMPOWERING GROUPS

The outline below shows how to develop successful groups (whether small or large, committees, boards, meetings, teams, etc.) that function well together and will get results done in a timely fashion.

- Meeting Notices
    - Open to the public.
        - Make sure people know this in advance.
    - Legally required to be posted in advance.
        - Newspapers – make the legal deadline or you can't legally meet.
        - On-site notices of agenda and other legal requirements. Also, note if limited time for the public to speak is allowed. State the time limit.
    - Sent out to committee, group, or board members prior to the meeting.
        - Send packets with information to members ahead of time.
        - Allow time for this to be mailed, received, and read before the meeting.
        - This can include subcommittee reports, past minutes, an agenda, budget, etc.
        - The main item is it saves enormous amounts of time at the meeting and people come to the meeting prepared.
        - With the digital age, some groups are doing this electronically. MAKE SURE your bylaws allow this to be done and everyone has access!
- Starting & ending times
    - Stick to them!
    - If you start late your credibility spirals downhill fast.
- Meeting rules
    - Make sure they are stated and everyone understands them.
    - A great method is to use Robert's Rules of Order, or at least a relaxed method of these rules.

- Above all MAKE SURE PEOPLE TURN OFF THEIR CELL PHONES.

- Officers – If you are on a board, council, organization, etc.
    - Make sure offices, and their respective duty descriptions, are in your approved Bylaws.
    - If a large formal meeting/group you will need the following:
        - President
        - Vice-President
        - Secretary - keeps a written record of ideas
        - Treasurer (Option, if needed.)
        - Historian (Option, if needed.)
        - Committee heads, assigned by the President or group leader.
- Committee Reporting
    - In the various State, Region, and Local Boards I have been on the following may be a time saver:
        - Once a committee is formed make sure they know their assigned task.
        - Make sure they know their deadlines.
            - DO NOT WAIT until the final committee deadline to find out problems they had, lack of results, dysfunctions of the committee, etc.
            - Require updates from the committee head at every meeting.
                - They may need more Board input or help.
    - It is also helpful to have a short reporting form for them to use.
        - You will find this method saves a lot of time and debate during meetings.
        - Put your trust in your committee. Your group will have the final say when they vote. You can accept their work or send it back for revisions.

Committee Head:
Committee Members:
Task:
Brief background:
Final Recommendation(s):
Date Submitted:
Sent back for revision: (Include brief reasons)
Approved:
Date:

- Room conditions
    - Tables, chairs
    - Table layouts
        - Even the major world powers can't agree on this one.
            - Remember back to the "Cold War" days when the United States delegation met for the first time with the Soviet Union. Months were spent trying to configure table layouts so that no one had control of the room and thus the meeting.
        - For our purposes, it depends on the size of the meeting you are holding. Go with whatever is functional.
    - Refer to the Appendix sections that include:
        - Lighting
        - Sound
        - Heating/air conditioning/air circulation/noise level / can it be adjusted
        - Podium
        - Microphone
        - Amenities – coffee, tea, water, pop, juice, cookies, etc.
    - Costs for room & food
    - Meeting locations
        - Free
        - Cost involved
        - Negotiate
            - May get the meeting room free if people eat lunch at the facility (motel, conference center, etc.)
    - Time factor
        - Preregister to get the facility
        - Do you need a key
        - Can you lock the room up if you go for lunch
        - How early can you set up
            - Do you have to wait for another group to leave & what if they run overtime?
            - Do you have to be out by a certain time?
            - Can you get a State/Government rate if your group belongs to a school district, local government, etc.?

    - Handouts
- Technology
    - Computer access
    - Internet access
    - Telephone access & cost
    - Projection Screen
    - Overhead (Yes, some people still use them.)
    - Video Projector
        - Can you bring your own in or do you have to rent something from the facility?
    - TV / VCR / DVD player /iPod /Laptop
    - Enough electrical outlets
    - Phone/ Internet connection (does this cost & does it have to be activated in advance?) Any bandwidth issues - other meetings going on at the same time.
    - Is a copy machine handy?
    - Is a fax machine handy? If still used.
    - Can you do a conference call if needed?
        - By phone
        - By Skype, webcam, or similar technology
        - Is it included in your By-Laws
    - Keep current (Be cautious of privacy issues):
        - Blog
        - Twitter
        - Facebook
        - Instagram

APPENDIX A: ROOM ENVIRONMENT

Sometimes controlling the meeting room environment can create a similar relaxing/less threatening feeling.

- Is the room well lit
- Does it have comfortable seating
- Is it quiet?
- Is the room temperature "just" right?

Rooms too hot or
Too cold tends to be a big distracter

- If the rooms or hallways nearby are noisy then you have a harder time hearing or being heard.

Other environmental factors such as bright sunlight cascading into the meeting room may mean you have to squint. It may also wash out visual presentation. Too dark a room may mean people may tend to doze off more easily. Nearby odors if unpleasant (dumpsters, too much perfume, or too strong an aftershave by someone sitting near you) also distract people. Does the heating/air conditioning unit overwhelm the room with a loud noise when it kicks in? Is there enough air circulation? Too little and people get sluggish.

I once was at a conference where the site was having the roof re-tarred. The foul odor was making everyone sick. This was unknown to the original committee that worked out arrangements with the site managers. Needless to say, this business site never got any more business from our State organization. Unfortunately, this resulted in the loss of future business and had an impact on this site for being less than honest.

However, many environmental factors can be controlled. Check with the building management to see if thermostats can be adjusted, if windows can be opened, if blinds can be drawn, and other useful ways to control your room environment as you prepare for a meeting. If not, see if you can find a better location that improves your chances of holding a successful group meeting.

Think in terms of your other senses as well. Some people may have trouble hearing or seeing depending on where they are sitting.

- You may think you have a strong voice but that does not mean everyone can hear you clearly!
    - Think in terms of other noises you hear when no one is talking

        - Heating or air condition units - are they too noisy?
        - Are your overhead lights buzzing?
        - Does the room echo?
        - Can you easily hear paper shuffling, and people talking, and does this interfere?
        - Are other people visiting (this can distract others and make it hard to hear you)
- Are you showing visuals?
    - Do you need a computer, video projector, document camera, television, or…?
    - Make sure your visuals can be seen adequately by your group. If not, can chairs be turned easily so people can comfortably follow along with the presentation?
    - Can you adjust the lighting so that your visuals can still be seen?
        - Are people still able to take notes?
        - CHECK THIS OUT AHEAD OF TIME!
            - Practice, practice, and practice to make sure everything is working! Nothing sours the tone of a meeting faster than wasting time on problems that should have been dealt with ahead of time.

HINT: Show up early and have everything set up and tried out! Nothing ruins a meeting faster than having the person in charge not being organized and ready.

Rule #1: Make sure the equipment works ahead of time!
Rule #2: When in doubt follow Rule #1

****

THE HINDSIGHT FILE

Or gee why didn't somebody tell me!

- If you are meeting at a hotel or conference center you can sometimes get your meeting room for FREE.
  - If your group has the facility to provide lunch on site and/or provide refreshments such as coffee, tea, and soda, plus snacks for a meeting break, the management often will provide the room free of charge.
  - This will make your group happy and content.
  - It will also provide income to the facility and staff serving you.
  - BUT, make sure you budgeted for this ahead of time!

APPENDIX B: AV EQUIPMENT NEEDS

- Do you need a microphone? 
    - If so, make sure you have access to the controls to lower or turn up the volume!
        - Or, have someone from the facility nearby to make the needed adjustment
        - Having a microphone not working shows little respect for your group
        - Setting volume detracts from the meeting and takes up valuable time
        - Problems with too little volume or with feedback (the high squelching noise you get if the microphone is facing an AV speaker, or turned up too much.)

 **HINTS:**

1. A corded microphone solves many problems BUT you have an annoying cable in the way. You are also tethered to how far you can move.
2. A wireless microphone is better if of decent quality. A "poor quality" microphone makes the clarity of voices hard to understand.
3. Always have fresh batteries for a wireless microphone so that it doesn't go out on you during the meeting.
4. NEVER use rechargeable batteries on a wireless microphone. You may hear differently but this is where experience rules! Rechargeable batteries have less power and your wireless microphone may not work.
5. Some wireless microphones "have" channel settings. If it doesn't work in practice, have someone double-check the channel settings. Preferably someone who knows the sound system and not a random busboy.

- Projection Screen
    - You have several options available
        - See if the facility has a screen in the "room" you are using
            - If you can't bring in your own equipment then you may have to rent from the facility

- Do they have a "drop-down screen" from the ceiling?
    - Is it powered so that you can flip a switch so that it can be lowered or raised?
    - Or do you have to find someone that is tall enough to pull it down? (Or do they have something to hook the handle to pull it down?)
    - It might already exist on the wall or hidden by a cupboard door – check ahead of time to make sure.
- An alternative might be to have a large-screen television on a wall that can be used.
    - Make sure it will accept cables so that you can use a computer, PowerPoint presentations, live video, etc.
    - Sometimes a set can be wheeled in on a cart
        - Make sure your equipment can be hooked up to it
        - ALSO, make sure you have access to enough electric outlets for all of your equipment.

    HINT: Make sure it can handle all your equipment without blowing a fuse. If not, make sure a staff member knows where the circuit breaker is and can reset it. They may also need a key to open the circuit breaker box.

- Laptop
    - If you are using a laptop, make sure you have all the proper cables to hook it up to a video projector or flat-screen TV.
    - If you are borrowing, or renting, a laptop, make sure you have the correct cables and connectors that fit the laptop.
        - Warning: I've been to meetings where most of the presentation was taken up trying to get the needed cables to make everything work.
        - Also, if you are using a remote control make sure you have fresh batteries. How many of you have been through this experience?

- Video Projector
  - This is a great tool for meetings and group presentations.
  - Some video projectors have a zoom lens that lets you fill the screen with images.
    - The larger the viewing area the easier it is for the audience to see and understand your graphics and data presented.

- Other equipment
  - If you need a 16mm projector, a filmstrip projector, a slide projector, a super 8mm projector, an 8mm loop projector, or an overhead projector.... RUN!
  - Unless this is to show archival material it is OUTDATED for a presentation today.
    - If you still choose to do so then make sure you have the proper mimeographed handouts to share. Or, for those of us that are old enough flashback to the hectograph handouts.
  - Some people still use overhead projectors but this means they don't have the right technology or aren't skilled enough to use it.
    - In this case, the presentations can be sloppy and the overhead transparency sheets can be poorly designed, overcrowded with information, and hard to read. It can also mean they don't have the budget.
    - With a computer, it is much easier to use PowerPoint presentations.
      - You can add graphics, pictures, charts, transitions, video, music, animation, etc. to make the presentations more vibrant and relevant.
        - "DON'T" overdo PowerPoint. We see a lot of it these days. Unless you are directing a movie, keep the presentations on task.
      - There are several options instead of using PowerPoint. Check with your associates as to other ideas.

- CD/DVD player (or newer technology)
  - CDs and/or DVDs are great for storing presentations.
  - Make sure this equipment is compatible with the video projector you are using. Some video projectors need to search for signals from the computer or other devices. Thumb drives are also handy if your computer or video projector can access them.
    - HINT: Make sure you know how to switch over to different equipment if needed. If not, you will lose your audience and credibility quickly.

- MP3 Player, Smartphones, iPads, iPads, and more
  - If using these devices make sure they can be hooked up to the video project, the flat-screen television, or your computer.
  - Nowadays, many items are wireless. If you are using such devices make sure they work and are compatible with the equipment you are using or renting.

- Internet
  - Do you have internet access?
    - Does this cost extra?
    - Do you need a special code to gain access?
    - How fast is this connection? Do downloads take forever?
      - HINT: It is smart to have your information stored on your computer, on a thumb drive, or on a DVD for faster access.

            - That way you avoid problems with downloading information via the Internet.
        - Can the audio presentation be heard clearly by all?
            - If not, get maintenance staff on it right away!
            - Have someone at the site who is familiar with the network, and internet protocols, on speed dial so you can get to them in a hurry if problems arise.
                - Again, how many of you have been at meetings and have tons of precious time wasted trying to get internet access?

- Added features
    - If you want to add people to your group (such as outside experts, members who couldn't attend in person, or site visits) you might want to use Skype.
        - This allows the opportunity to reach beyond borders.
            - Example: When a Wisconsin professor was stranded in Iceland due to volcanic ash, which closed the airports, he was able to use Skype to meet with his students in Wisconsin.
    - Microsoft's GO TO MEETING is another excellent example of "two-way teleconferencing" for group meetings.
    - Explore other products. Remember that there are also options such as "Drop Boxes" to share information, pictures, handouts, etc. Different programs call them different names.
        - During online meetings, the control person/speaker can also control video links with participants, show video, and printed documents, control microphones online (on/off, especially if a microphone is noisy or distracting the group), and take offline questions.
    - Technology is changing fast and improving.
    - sDon't forget Webinars (online live video presentations).
        - If participating from home you are at the mercy of the internet speed you have available.

****

THE HINDSIGHT FILE

It is often handy to have access to a photocopier when you have a meeting.

- If you have handouts often you run out.
- You may need to share notes with the groups.
- Some unexpected need is expressed and the photocopier is needed.

APPENDIX C: INTRODUCING NEW MEMBERS

How many times have you been the new person being added, or replacing, a current group member?

- How comfortable were you?
- Were you nervous?
- Were you confused as to why you were asked to be a member?
- Do you ask yourself, "Oh, Oh? I don't really fit in with these talented people?"
- Before the meeting started did you smile and introduce yourself?

How did the members of the group/meeting find out about you?

- Did the Chair/Leader introduce you to the group?
- Did s/he ask you to briefly talk about yourself?
- Did s/he mention why you were being added?
  - This could include your expertise and experience.
  - It could be you represent a certain location in the region or state or some other demographic.
- Did other members offer a friendly greeting, with introductions of themselves?
- Remember first impressions make a difference – you cannot redo it again.

Did the leader ask other members to introduce themselves to you?

- This can be time-consuming but at least you know who these people are, where they are from, and why they are there.
- Good luck if it is a large group remembering who is who.
- At one meeting our leader asked each of us instead to mention something fun we did over the summer.
  - This really opened up conversations and gave us insights into our co-workers.
  - To get people co-operating and involved you might use a deck of cards and pass out one to each person. Depending on the size of the group you could have all the "2's" get together and so on. Or have them breakdown by "suits of cards"

Then have each mini-group interview each other.

- Have a selected group of questions to ask.

- Name, hobby, favorite travel place, etc.
    - Set a time limit and then have the whole group reassemble.
    - Have a team leader from each group do a mini rundown as to what they learned from their mini-group.
- To select a team leader/reporter
    - Have them draw cards – the highest number wins.
    - Roll dice – the highest combination wins the job.
    - Ask for birthdates – the closest to your meeting date wins.

APPENDIX D: OTHER USEFUL INFORMATION

Quick Guide for Effective Groups - Review

In past meetings do any of “these sound” familiar?

- Group meetings are time-draining encounters in which little gets accomplished.
  Yes No
- You’re responsible for leading a team, but you don’t have any supervisory authority.
  Yes No
- Not all team members understand the role they play on the team.
  Yes No
- Your team is composed of people from diverse backgrounds (age, gender, race, etc.) and you sometimes have trouble relating to them.
  Yes No
- Some team members consistently don’t pull their own weight.
  Yes No
- Some of the team members don’t get along – and it’s impacting the team’s effectiveness.
  Yes No
- You’re dealing with a stubborn team member who thinks it is his/her way and will not listen to other views.
  Yes No
- Some individuals want to be solo heroes instead of team players.
  Yes No

APPENDIX E: USEFUL EXCUSES AND TACTICS

If you can't annoy somebody, there is little point in writing – Kingsley Amis

Never get into fights with ugly people because they have nothing to lose – unknown

I get my exercise acting as a pallbearer to my friends who exercise – Chauncy Depew (1834-1938)
Ok, so maybe it doesn't fit but I like it anyway.

Never go to a doctor whose office plants have died – Erma Bomback

I might have gone to West Point, but I was too proud to speak to a Congressman – Will Rogers (1879-1933)

Smoking is one of the leading causes of statistics – Fletcher Kennel

A statesman is a politician who has been dead for ten or fifteen years – Harry S. Truman (1889-1972)

TRIVIA

Did you know...

That you don't have to be tall to be a leader?

- Napoleon Bonaparte was 5'5" tall
- Attila the Hun was only 3'5" in height
    - Surprised me as well, but check it out.

- Ludwig van Beethoven was 5'3"
- Pablo Picasso was 5'4"

- Harry Houdini was 5'4"
- Mahatma Gandhi was 5'5"
- Nikita Khrushchev, a Soviet Leader, was 5'3"
- Charlotte Bronte, English Novelist and Poet, was 4'10"
- Andre Carnegie was 5'3"

- James Madison, U.S. President, was 5'5"

NOT SO TYPICAL BIBLIOGRAPHY

Office.com Clip Art – Royalty-free photos and illustrations

- Except for my photograph, all artwork is from Office.com Clip Art
- Feel free to enlarge my photograph and frame it – it makes a great dart board.

Howard Gardner

- Use the following terms for Internet research
  - Howard + Gardner
  - Howard + Gardner + Multiple + Intelligence + Theories
  - Howard + Gardner + Multiple + Intelligence + Test
  - Howard + Gardner + Multiple + Intelligence + Chart

Leadership

- Use the following terms for Internet research
  - Leadership
  - Leadership + Skills
  - Leadership + Training
  - Leadership + Styles
  - Leadership + Versus + Management

If you are interested in these and other topics check your local library and bookstores for other beneficial resources.

I purposely created an "interactive" bibliography so you would be forced to test (or double-check) my reasoning and thought processes. Plus, this adds to your wealth of knowledge either proving or trying to disprove my ideas. Either way, you win!

ABOUT THE AUTHOR

Frederick Marini

Born in Baraboo, Wisconsin
Currently resides near Melrose, Wisconsin

- Retired Educator: District Media Director/Librarian/Teacher, PreK-12
- Author: Ghosts of the Past, Action/Adventure Book
- Author: Family, Food, & Fun, a family cookbook and family history
- Inventor: EZ Step Ladder / EZ Step Stool for handicapped & injured access

Previous History & Involvements on Boards/Committees

- Wisconsin Library Service (WILS) – State Board
- Wisconsin Library Service & Technology (LSTA) – State Advisory Board
- WWBIC (Western Wisconsin Broadcasting Instructional Council) Advisory Board
- WWBIC -TAC (Teachers' Advisory Council)
- Member of WEA, NEA, CRUE, MMAEA & AAA (sorry got carried away with letters). All except AAA were professional teacher unions.
- State Superintendent Award 2011 "Standing Up for Rural Wisconsin Schools, Libraries, and Communities"
- Received the first Follett / WEMA Library Service Award for Wisconsin
- Served several terms as a Board of Director for the Wisconsin Education Media Association (WEMA), now called the Wisconsin Education Media and Technology Association (WEMTA)
    - Former State Leadership Chair
    - Served on several planning committees for WEMA State Media Conferences
    - State Chair for several Summer WEMA Leadership Conferences

- Past President of the Melrose-Mindoro Educational Association (MMAEA)
- Past President Winding Rivers Intertype Steering Council (long time ago)
- Work experience in various school districts, Public Library, & with the University of Wisconsin
- Also taught Adult Ed. Courses through WWTC (Western Wisconsin Technical College)
- La Crosse County Library Board – Past Board Member/Trustee & Secretary
- And much more but I don't want to bore you.

www.ingramcontent.com/pod-product-compliance
Lightning Source LLC
LaVergne TN
LVHW071220220926
848486LV00037B/279

* 9 7 9 8 8 9 4 9 9 2 7 4 7 *